BRINGING BACK OUR
DESERTS

BY CLARA MacCARALD

CONTENT CONSULTANT

Sergio Avila-Villegas, M.Sc.
Conservation Biologist

Essential Library

An Imprint of Abdo Publishing
abdopublishing.com

CONSERVATION
SUCCESS STORIES

abdopublishing.com

Published by Abdo Publishing, a division of ABDO, PO Box 398166, Minneapolis, Minnesota 55439. Copyright © 2018 by Abdo Consulting Group, Inc. International copyrights reserved in all countries. No part of this book may be reproduced in any form without written permission from the publisher. Essential Library™ is a trademark and logo of Abdo Publishing.

Printed in the United States of America, North Mankato, Minnesota
092017
012018

Cover Photo: iStockphoto
Interior Photos: Eric Foltz/iStockphoto, 4; iStockphoto, 6, 11, 68, 85, 86, 99 (top); Lutsenko Larissa/Shutterstock Images, 8–9, 98 (bottom left); Shutterstock Images, 15 (left), 15 (right), 16, 54, 94–95; Anton Petrus/Shutterstock Images, 19; Jim Zipp/Science Source, 22; Grant Hellman Photography/Alamy, 23; John R. Foster/Science Source, 27; Pavel Tvrdy/Shutterstock Images, 28; Neil Lockhart/iStockphoto, 30; Andre van der Veen/Shutterstock Images, 32; Joseph Sohm/Shutterstock Images, 34; znm/iStockphoto, 36; Zack Frank/Shutterstock Images, 38; Everett Collection Inc/Alamy, 41; Arnoud Quanjer/Shutterstock Images, 44; Stocktrek Images/Alamy, 45; Nature and Science/Alamy, 46; Rick & Nora Bowers/Alamy, 50; Jonah Photos/iStockphoto, 51; Houshmand Rabbani/Shutterstock Images, 52–53; Milosz Maslanka/Shutterstock Images, 55; P. J. Sells/iStockphoto, 58–59, 98 (bottom right); Janelle Lugge/Shutterstock Images, 61; Ilona Ignatova/Shutterstock Images, 63, 99 (bottom); Christian Prohaska/iStockphoto, 65; Eric Celebrezze/Shutterstock Images, 69; Neil Lockhart/Shutterstock Images 70, 98 (top right); AfriPics.com/Alamy, 72; Zuma Press, Inc/Alamy, 74; Nature's Images/Science Source, 75; California Dreamin/Alamy, 77; Van der Meer Marica/Arterra Picture Library/Alamy, 80; Robert Ford/iStockphoto, 82; Jonathan Pledger/Shutterstock Images, 84; Adam Kaz/iStockphoto, 88; Durk Talsma/iStockphoto, 91; ESB Professional/Shutterstock Images, 93; Aurora Photos/Alamy, 96

Editor: Alyssa Krekelberg
Series Designer: Laura Polzin

Publisher's Cataloging-in-Publication Data

Names: MacCarald, Clara, author.
Title: Bringing back our deserts / by Clara MacCarald.
Description: Minneapolis, Minnesota : Abdo Publishing, 2018. | Series: Conservation success stories | Includes online resources and index.
Identifiers: LCCN 2017946749 | ISBN 9781532113130 (lib.bdg.) | ISBN 9781532152016 (ebook)
Subjects: LCSH: Desert conservation--Juvenile literature. | Restoration ecology--Juvenile literature. | Conservation of natural resources--Juvenile literature.
Classification: DDC 333.736--dc23
LC record available at https://lccn.loc.gov/2017946749

CONTENTS

The Joshua tree's survival depends on well-timed rainfall.

JOSHUA TREE NATIONAL PARK

In southern California, the mountainous Mojave Desert meets and mingles with the low-lying Sonoran Desert in Joshua Tree National Park (JTNP). The park protects 1,238 square miles (3,207 sq km)—an area larger than the state of Rhode Island.[1] Despite the harsh conditions, the park supports a diverse array of plant life.

Hundreds of plants live in JTNP. Many of those plants are wildflowers that paint the low-lying areas of the park in dazzling displays after spring rains, drawing hundreds of thousands of tourists. Humans are not the only visitors. More than 250 bird species have been recorded in JTNP, though only 78 of those stay in the park to breed.[2] Others stop over during migration for rest and refreshment, and some

NORTH AMERICAN DESERTS

Four major deserts cover vast territories in North America. Though all are dry, location and rainfall patterns have lent different characteristics to each. The Sonoran Desert stretches from southern Arizona and California down into Mexico. Its mild winters and sporadic summer downpours nurture a diverse mix of temperate and tropical plant species. The colder and slightly wetter Mojave Desert covers an area from southern California north to Nevada, Arizona, and Utah. The Chihuahuan Desert reaches farthest south, from southern New Mexico and Texas and into Mexico, although it frequently suffers freezes in winters because of its high elevation. The cold Great Basin Desert is the highest and farthest north of the four. With parts reaching south into Arizona and New Mexico, it also stretches north to Oregon and Idaho.

wander in from nearby mountains to escape periods of heavy snow. The park also provides homes for 52 species of mammals, 44 species of reptiles, and two species of amphibians.[3] It also has a vast number of arthropods, including 75 species of butterflies.[4]

RESTORING THE DESERT

JTNP's land was dotted with hundreds of mines, which were created by prospectors in the 1800s. Native plants struggled to grow throughout much of the area. Some areas had been stripped by miners for fuel and for mining props, while others had been cleared by homesteaders for unsuccessful attempts at dryland farming. Hundreds of miles of roads snaked through the desert. People could easily drive into sensitive areas where they might trample or steal unique desert plants. Traffic also brought seeds from non-native plants.

In the 1970s, managers started tackling challenges in JTNP, beginning with the tamarisk tree, an invasive species. Originally from Eurasia, tamarisk was deliberately planted by gardeners and landscapers to make windbreaks and shade. These trees' roots drink from deep underground, stealing water from native species and leaching salt into the soil.

JTNP staff trekked far and wide throughout the national park to destroy tamarisks that had found their way to many remote springs and oases. Soon managers added new targets, such as Asian mustard, tumbleweed, and invasive grasses. These non-native grasses include fountain grass, which outcompetes native bunch grasses, and two grasses that feed large fires in areas that are not adapted to burn. Over time, people at JTNP have removed thousands of invasive plants, freeing springs in the park from both tamarisks and fountain grass.

Getting rid of unwanted species is one part of restoration, but another key step is returning native species. Pieces of land in JTNP had never fully recovered from the destruction wrought by miners and homesteaders. Early attempts to replant old gravel pits stalled as seeds struggled to germinate and

HISTORY OF JTNP

In the 1920s, Pasadena, California, resident Minerva Hoyt became concerned by the loss of desert vegetation to cactus poachers. These poachers snatched cacti from the desert and sold them for cactus gardens in places like Los Angeles. Hoyt started a conservation movement that led to the establishment of what was then the Joshua Tree National Monument in 1936. In 1976, the government designated approximately 80 percent of the monument as wilderness, protected from further roads and mechanized vehicles.[5] In 1994, a growing awareness of the desert as a unique and valuable ecosystem led to the California Desert Protection Act. Along with increased protections for other deserts, the act changed Joshua Tree from a national monument into a national park and expanded it to its current size. Since 2009, 85 percent of JTNP is classified as wilderness.

"Viewed from the roadside, the dry land only hints at hidden vitality, but closer examination reveals a giant mosaic of an ecosystem, intensely beautiful and complex."[6]

—A description of JTNP from National Parks of the American West

seedlings frequently died. Without better methods, JTNP had no hope of rehabilitating large areas. The staff started the Center for Arid Lands Restoration (CALR) in 1986 to research and develop new restoration techniques. They found that desert plants survived better when they were started in the nursery before being transplanted into arid conditions.

In the 1990s, JTNP began to close roads throughout the park. Along with spreading invasive species, roads favor traffic, which becomes a threat for wildlife such as the desert tortoise. Eventually, more than 167 miles (269 km) were retired from active use.[7] To disguise closed roads from drivers who might be tempted to turn down them, staff concentrated their work near intersections. At some intersections, they rehabilitated the desert with pitting and vertical mulching. Pitting is creating holes in the soil that help trap water from infrequent desert rains. Vertical mulching is a technique of burying dead plant material upright in the soil, which often blends

Tamarisk trees thrive in habitats around water.

9

CENTER FOR ARID LANDS RESTORATION

In the 1980s, few nurseries sold mature plants from the Mojave Desert—there just wasn't a market. So when JTNP wanted native specimens to restock sites around the park, they had to supply their own. They started with a small nursery. By 1992, the nursery had expanded and included two greenhouses and the capacity to grow thousands of native plants. The Center for Arid Lands Restoration (CALR) was the name they gave to all the plant-related programs at JTNP, including the nursery, restoration program, and rare plant research. CALR not only benefited JTNP, but also came to supply state, federal, and private organizations with rare plants and expertise.

"The years following Joshua Tree's promotion to national park status have been marked by more popularity, a higher worldwide profile, improved scientific management of resources, and more respect from senior agency officials."[9]

—Lary Dilsaver, Professor Emeritus of Geography at the University of South Alabama, 2015

in with the live vegetation and helps the land catch water, soil, and seeds.

JTNP started relocating roads and creating new parking lots to manage the impact of tourists, leading to new areas being cleared. Rather than lose plants that had been nurtured by the desert, the staff learned to salvage live plants for restoration work in other areas. Every year, vegetation crews continue to attack invasive species while spreading and nurturing natives.

THE FUTURE OF JTNP

Trails at JTNP lead visitors to features such as the Lost Palms Oasis and the Lost Horse Mine, a remnant of mining in the park. The desert may appear timeless, but it has always changed, with the rate of change accelerating in the last couple of hundred years. The desert would not look so beautiful without years of active, ongoing restoration.

Even as a protected area, JTNP is affected by human activities. The number of visitors increases every year, with more than 2.5 million in 2016.[8]

One trail at JTNP leads to the Cholla Cactus Garden.

Park managers are searching for ways to minimize the impacts of tourists on the natural wonders they've come to see, which may require adding additional entrances and a new visitor center.

JOSHUA TREES

Legends say early Mormon settlers gave Joshua trees their name because they imagined the trees looked like the biblical figure of Joshua welcoming them to a new land. But for modern visitors, these tall succulents likely evoke the scenery of a Dr. Seuss book. Towering up to 40 feet (12 m), Joshua trees are a tall species of yucca, a plant genus with 49 members.[10] Similar to many perennial desert plants, Joshua tree seeds sprout rarely, but adults live for a long time, averaging 150 years or more. Shallow but wide root networks take advantage of sudden downpours. Joshua trees provide nesting sites for dozens of bird species, but for its own reproduction it requires yucca moths. Without the moths to pollinate, there would be no new Joshua trees. While neither Joshua trees nor yucca moths are yet endangered, the Joshua tree faces threats from development and climate change.

Industrial and residential development continues to advance on the park's borders. On some days, air pollution from nearby cities reaches levels known to affect human health, which may also affect desert animals. Plants are vulnerable, too. One concern is that nitrogen from air pollution may fertilize the desert and favor non-native over native plants.

Climate change is starting to make itself known, with frequent droughts in the region already impacting the reproduction of Joshua trees. As the buildup of greenhouse gases warms the planet, the southwestern United States is predicted to become hotter and drier. Species will relocate to new areas or disappear completely. Managers at JTNP are considering strategies for monitoring the effects of climate change and actions to protect vulnerable species and ecosystems in the park. With continued work, JTNP will be home to a diverse array of native desert species and landscapes of startling beauty for decades to come.

CONSERVATION SUCCESSES IN THE DESERT

From a human perspective, the desert is a harsh environment, yet it teems with life in unexpected places. Though these organisms survive extreme conditions, they don't always adjust well to changes brought on by human activities. The human footprint on desert lands has been vast and transformative. Agriculture, roads, development, pollution, and invasive species still threaten deserts around the world, as they have for much of recent history. New challenges such as climate change have come with the expansion of human populations and new technology.

Along with big challenges, deserts have also been the site of big conservation successes, such as JTNP. The park is a beautiful desert land protected from many human disturbances, with much of the destructive impact of invasive species controlled and many sites restored by native plantings. Other degraded deserts around the world have also been protected and restored, thanks to the work of conservationists, land managers, governments, and others. The deserts of the future will not be the same as those that existed before modern agriculture and development, but they can be functioning ecosystems that continue to support a variety of unique life-forms.

NITROGEN POLLUTION

Every living thing needs nitrogen. The element is an essential component of proteins, which are organic compounds that perform many cell functions. It is also part of nucleic acids, which are the compounds that code genetic information in the cell. Earth's atmosphere is 78 percent nitrogen, but most organisms can't use atmospheric nitrogen.[11] Nitrogen-fixing microbes are an exception. They pull nitrogen from the atmosphere and fix it into specific compounds such as ammonium that living organisms can use. Some nitrogen-fixing microbes form symbiotic relationships with plant roots.

In most deserts, low nitrogen is the largest factor limiting plant growth. While native desert plants are adapted to grow in a low-nitrogen environment, air pollution is increasing nitrogen in soils near developed areas. Nitrogen can arrive as particles in the air or ride to the ground with precipitation.

Some parts of JTNP receive high levels of nitrogen from urban areas to the west, particularly from the Los Angeles basin. This nitrogen increases soil fertility. Scientists fear fast-growing invasive species are better equipped to take advantage of this windfall than desert natives. One study in JTNP, led by a professor at the University of California, Riverside, found that added nitrogen did increase the growth of non-native grasses. The results in native plants varied. In some cases, it also stimulated the growth of native plants. Other times, native plants decreased because of competition with fast-growing non-natives.

NITROGEN CYCLE

Atmospheric Nitrogen

Nitrogen Fixing

Ammonium

Many plants receive the nitrogen they need from the soil.

According to the United Nations, deserts and semideserts cover approximately 17 percent of Earth's land surface.

Chapter
TWO

WHAT IS
A DESERT?

Deserts are dry lands. To qualify as a desert, the rate water is added to an ecosystem must be less than that which leaves through evaporation. The exact number differs by location, but in general arid deserts receive less than 10 inches (25 cm) of precipitation per year.[1] Lands with 10 to 20 inches (25 to 50 cm) of precipitation are still dry and are usually classified as semiarid.[2]

Ultimately, dry air creates deserts. This dry air may be caused by one of several global or geological features. Bands of dry winds straddle both sides of the equator and produce several major deserts, including the Sahara and three of the American deserts: the Mojave, Sonoran, and Chihuahuan. Ocean circulation

DESERT EXTREMES

The Sahara is the largest desert in the world at 3.5 million square miles (9.1 million sq km).[3] It's nearly the size of the continental United States. The hottest desert is Death Valley in California's Mojave Desert, where, during a heat wave in 1913, people recorded a temperature of 134 degrees Fahrenheit (57°C), the highest air temperature ever recorded on Earth as of 2017.[4] At the southern end of the world, Antarctica, the largest cold desert, stretches for 5 million square miles (13 million sq km). It holds the record for the lowest recorded temperature, -128.6 degrees Fahrenheit (-89.2°C).[5] Some scientists believe the Namib Desert in southern Africa is the oldest desert, having little to no rain for millions of years or more.

also makes deserts. On the western edges of certain continents, frigid water wells up from deep below the sea and cools the air passing overhead. Cold air holds less moisture than warm air. The Atacama in South America, which is the driest desert in the world, and the Namib in Africa are known as coastal deserts.

There are also deserts deep in the interior of continents, such as the Gobi Desert in Asia. When the air from the ocean reaches these deserts, it has traveled so far that it has lost most of its moisture. These deserts are also far from the temperature moderating effects of the ocean, causing them to experience great extremes in air temperature from summer to winter. Other deserts lie in a rain shadow, as both the Mojave and Great Basin Desert do. An air mass coming off the ocean rises over a mountain range and cools, which makes it drop most of its water as precipitation. When the air sinks back down on the other side of the mountains, it warms up, holds tight to remaining moisture, and creates a dry shadow.

The Gobi Desert is the largest desert in Asia.

DIVERSITY IN DRY LANDS

Deserts can look and act very different from each other, even though they all share a lack of water. Deserts are found on every continent, and their climates vary greatly. Not all deserts are hot. Barren valleys in frozen Antarctica classify as deserts. Some deserts have very cold winters, while even the hottest deserts may be chilly at night since they lack water vapor or cloud cover to hold in the heat. But during the day, air temperatures in hot deserts can surge to more than 100 degrees Fahrenheit (38°C), even in winter.[6]

"In addition to being meager, desert precipitation is also highly variable and unpredictable. The more arid the desert, the more variable is its rainfall."[7]

—The Arizona-Sonora Desert Museum

Different deserts typically experience precipitation in different seasons. For a desert's vegetation, the time of year in which precipitation comes is almost as important as how much falls. Coastal deserts may experience very little life-giving water except what settles as fog. Some researchers claim the Atacama Desert lacked rain for a period of hundreds of years.

Ground cover differs among deserts. Many deserts have scattered plants, but some have no visible life at all. Some deserts drown in shifting sand dunes. A type of ground cover called desert pavement forms over thousands of years as a layer of rocks covers the soil. Some deserts have crusts teeming with microscopic life, which is called a biological or cryptobiotic soil crust. Even the extremely dry Atacama Desert has microorganisms clinging in the pores between rocks.

DESERT ADAPTATIONS

Unless the ground is overwhelmed by shifting dunes or scoured to bare rock by the wind, most deserts have some plants. But no plant can live completely without water, and desert plants deal with arid conditions in different ways. Some plants wait out dry periods as seeds, including many wildflowers such as the Arizona lupine. When water comes, these annuals germinate and complete their life cycle quickly. Perennials like creosote bush might grow slowly, but they live for a long time. Because of their longer lives, perennials need to survive arid conditions as adults. Many types of desert shrubs such as brittlebush drop their leaves during dry periods. Creosote bushes do not lose their waxy leaves, but they become so dry as to appear dead.

Not all desert plants are at the mercy of the weather. Succulents avoid drying out by storing water in fleshy stems or leaves. Some desert plants send their roots deep underground to find the water table. Mesquite tree roots, for example, might dig down

"When enough rain finally does fall, [wildflowers] quickly sprout, grow, bloom and go back to seed again before the dryness and heat returns. By blooming together during good years, wildflowers can attract large numbers of pollinators such as butterflies, moths, bees and hummingbirds that might not otherwise visit Death Valley."[8]

—*Death Valley National Park*

SUCCULENTS

Succulents are plants with fleshy stems or leaves that store water. North American succulents include both the familiar cactus and the Joshua tree. Africa has ice plants, whose white-tinged leaves look iced despite the heat, and stone plants, which resemble the rocks and pebbles among which they live. Most succulents have wide, shallow root systems to capture rain and waxy skin to keep from drying out. Like other desert plants, some succulents are protected by spikes or spines. Many succulents stop water loss in an additional way. While most plants must open their pores during the day to capture carbon dioxide for photosynthesis, these plants can catch carbon dioxide at night when low temperatures reduce water loss.

Kangaroo rats are found in dry regions of the southwestern and western United States.

more than 200 feet (60 m).[9] Desert roots like those of creosote can extend widely near the soil surface to rapidly soak up rainfall. Excessive evaporation can lead to a buildup of salts in desert soils. High salt levels are toxic for most plants. Some plants have adapted to deal with this problem by excreting salt, like tamarisk does, or by storing it in special structures, as does the common reed.

Animals can more easily seek out favorable conditions because of their mobility. Some animals migrate through, limiting the degree to which they experience desert conditions.

A wide variety of birds do so, from water fowl including wood ducks to song birds such as robins. Bats, including three species of leaf-nosed bats, use desert resources for migration by fueling up on nectar from cacti and agave flowers in the Sonoran Desert.

In hot deserts, animals beat the heat by finding shade or being nocturnal, often spending the day underground in cool and moist burrows. For example, kangaroo rats and pocket mice only emerge from their burrows at night. Fennec foxes use their large ears to lose heat from their bodies. Other animals become dormant during the hottest, driest parts of the year. Desert frogs and spadefoot toads spend most of the year in burrows. They only emerge to eat and breed during rainy periods.

Whether in a hot or cold desert, thirst is a problem. Many desert animals have reduced the amount of water they lose from their body surface. As an extreme example of water efficiency, kangaroo rats can obtain all the water they need from seeds without ever having to drink. Although camels must drink, they've

DESERT INVERTEBRATES

Small invertebrates play big roles in desert ecosystems. Tunnels made by ants and termites increase the amount of oxygen and water that can infiltrate the soil. Soil invertebrates like mites and nematodes also improve desert soils and provide food for larger animals. A vast number of species will snack on invertebrates, including birds, small rodents, lizards, snakes, and even animals as big as coyotes. Insects can suppress plant populations with their own appetites, and ants have even frustrated desert restoration studies by removing young seedlings.

AQUIFERS

Some aquifers hold vast stores of water under deserts, such as the ones below parts of the Sahara Desert and in areas of Australia. An aquifer does not contain an underground lake. Instead, water surrounds the rocks or other material, flowing through cracks or pores either quickly or very slowly. Aquifers may extend from the ground downward, or they may be trapped far underground by a layer of material resistant to water. When water is trapped, pressure can force it to the surface through cracks to make a water feature such as an oasis. Water removed from an aquifer may take a long time to replace, since the aquifer's water may have come from rain that fell a long distance away or that fell thousands of years ago.

earned their reputation as iconic desert animals by surviving extreme dehydration. Once they find water, they guzzle it down and rapidly rehydrate.

WATER IN THE DESERT

Although scarce, the water present in a desert helps shape the landscape and influence its ecology. When rain does arrive, it fills streams and rivers. If the rain is heavy enough, it forms sudden floods that sweep up everything in their paths and carve deep channels in the ground. Less dramatically, water can be found under most deserts in aquifers. An aquifer is a layer underground through which water can flow. Where underground water seeps to the surface as a spring, it creates wetlands and oases. When the ground dips down below the water table, lakes form. Depending on the material making up the aquifer, the water welling up may be too salty for all but salt-adapted plants.

Habitats that surround water are known as riparian habitats. Although riparian habitats only take up a small portion of the desert landscape, they support a rich diversity of vegetation and wildlife. Riparian areas sustain many species of conservation concern, such as the endangered Southwestern willow flycatcher. According to the Springs Stewardship

Desert rainstorms are rare, but they are important to the species living there.

Institute, springs specifically support 20 percent of endangered species across the United States.[10] The endangered desert pupfish, for example, lives in springs and streams in the southwestern United States and Mexico. Desert water sources also provide resources and rest areas for migrating birds such as geese and ducks.

CRYPTOBIOTIC CRUSTS

To humans, deserts often appear bleak, but in many places even the soil crust is alive. Cryptobiotic crusts are made by a mix of bacteria, algae, fungi, lichens, and plants. The name *cryptobiotic* comes from the cryptic nature of this soil life, which is hidden in plain sight from those who don't know about it. The crust often appears dark and dead when water is scarce, but it rehydrates quickly and turns green within minutes of rain falling.

Cryptobiotic crusts are sometimes known as desert glue. They knit the top of the soil together with root-like, sticky threads, keeping it from washing or blowing away. Soil organisms also increase soil fertility. They help water soak into the soil, and their presence adds organic matter and other nutrients. One nutrient they might add is nitrogen, which nitrogen-fixing bacteria pull from the air and fix into forms plants and other organisms can use.

Unfortunately, cryptobiotic crusts are fragile. When human activity crushes or removes soil crusts, deserts become more vulnerable to the forces of erosion. Sometimes patches of intact crust are left standing while the land erodes around them. After being damaged, cryptobiotic crusts may recover, depending on the availability of crust organisms in the nearby environment that can replenish the site, but full recovery takes a long time.

Cryptobiotic soil crusts are typically found in desert regions.

Roads through the desert harm native species.

Chapter
THREE

HUMAN FOOTPRINT IN THE DESERT

Humans have lived in deserts for a long time. Hunter-gatherers such as the Taaqtam (Serrano) tribe in the JTNP area skillfully used and managed desert resources to make a living. Nomadic herders moved their animals to take advantage of different areas and limit the effect of grazing on any one pasture, as Mongolian herders have done in the Gobi Desert during modern times. Ancient farmers, such

MINING

Many deserts hide commodities beneath their surface, such as water and minerals. For a long time, people have ventured into the desert looking to make their fortune without heeding their impact on the landscape. In the 1500s, the Spanish brought large-scale mining to the Chihuahuan Desert in Mexico. In the 1860s, prospectors forged into the deserts of the southwestern United States and trickled into the Australian desert. The 1872 Mining Act in the United States allowed settlers to legally take over American Indian tribal lands. Mining interests in the United States can still invoke the 1872 law to gain ownership of public land. In the 1900s, oil and gas were major lures. In 1912, an oil company exported the first batch of oil from a port on the Persian Gulf, heralding an oil boom that would spread across desert countries in North Africa and the Middle East in the middle of the century.

as those in the Negev Desert, used innovative methods of capturing water for irrigation to turn the desert into lush cropland.

Ancient desert dwellers did not always live peacefully within their ecosystems. Sometimes climate conditions changed, making previous methods of living unsustainable, as happened when the Sahara turned from a green land with lakes to a desert thousands of years ago. Other times human activity itself was to blame for changed conditions. Irrigation could lead to salty conditions in the soil, making farming difficult or impossible. This may have happened in Mashkan Shapir, a city in Mesopotamia abandoned around 1720 BCE as a result of war. Excessive grazing could strip an area entirely of plants or alter vegetation until only hardy goats or camels could survive, as happened in parts of what is now Jordan, a country in the Middle East.

In the modern era, colonizers looked at deserts first as dangerous, degenerate lands and later as wastelands ripe for exploitation. Deserts have been changed by waves of miners, settlers, and their livestock. Biodiversity has been lost and ecological processes disrupted by invasive species spread by human activities. Throughout the world, deserts have been damaged by human activity.

INTENSIVE LAND USE

Many deserts are grazed by livestock. Nomadic herds can be moved before they cause too much damage in one area, but herds forced to stay in one place will overgraze. Overgrazing does more than kill plants. It changes the plant community. Heavy grazing by cows can reduce the availability of tender forage, leading herders to graze hardier animals that can eat tougher plants. Herders move to sheep, goats, and finally camels as the vegetation becomes more and more formidable. By decimating native plants, livestock can help non-native species invade an area, which the yellow star thistle did in California after overgrazing by cows and sheep.

Overgrazing causes other changes to the environment. In deserts with a cryptobiotic soil crust, hooves trample the soil organisms and make the land both less productive and more prone to erosion. Grazing is particularly destructive in riparian areas. Livestock devastate lush riparian plant communities, eliminating important species. Water temperatures rise, and stream banks are destabilized. The water becomes polluted with manure and the bacteria it contains, as well as chemicals and nutrients washed off fertilized pastures.

As domestic animals strip away plants, the bare ground heats up and can actually decrease the amount of rain that falls over the area.

Often, livestock affect native species. They compete with native grazers such as bighorn sheep for food. Herders may control native predators such as wolves and mountain lions, increasing populations of prey such as deer and rabbits who then feed more heavily on desert plants. Herders might feed their livestock by spreading non-native plants, sometimes clearing large areas of native plants to do so. Some introduced species have spread and wreaked ecological havoc.

Desert agriculture can be productive and sustainable, which means capable of being maintained without causing ecological damage or resource depletion. It can also fail. After failing to grow crops in unsuitable soil without enough water, many farmers abandon their cleared land. Vegetation may not recover in these areas, even decades later. If farmers aren't careful with irrigation, their soil becomes salty or alkaline. When farmers pump too much irrigation water from aquifers, water tables drop and plant roots no longer reach moisture.

"By some estimates the severe overgrazing during droughts in the late 1800s cut the permanent grazing potential of California in half, and it is likely that the impact was even larger in the desert."[1]

—David A. Bainbridge, author of A Guide for Desert and Dryland Restoration

ENCROACHING DEVELOPMENT

Rural livelihoods have left a heavy mark on many deserts, but large-scale developments have been increasing their footprint in recent decades. As building booms reach into the desert landscapes, desert habitat becomes converted into urban and other residential

Housing developments have negatively affected desert biodiversity.

areas. In some cases, proposed subdivisions never materialize even though the land was cleared and the desert destroyed.

Some development has focused on extracting minerals, oil, and gas from under the desert floor. Development has meant the construction of roads, power lines, pipelines, overhead transmission lines, and canals. These developments destroy desert vegetation, threaten wildlife and their migratory patterns, provide people with access to sensitive desert habitat, and bring non-native seeds into new areas. Car exhaust and urban areas create pollution, such as nitrogen, ozone, and dust, which can alter desert habitats and damage vegetation.

Development also places pressure on desert water sources. People remove water from waterways and the ground to provide for growing communities—and sometimes for extravagancies such as desert golf courses. Water that flows from residential and industrial areas brings a group of nasty substances, including fecal bacteria, paint, pesticides, and medications. Pavement and other hard surfaces in urban areas increase runoff, leading to frequent severe

NATIVE MANAGEMENT

In places such as the southwestern United States and Australia, settlers changed the desert by displacing native peoples from parts of it. For example, three groups occupied JTNP before being forced out by European settlers: the Agua Caliente Band of Cahuilla Indians (Cahuilla), Chemehuevi Indian Tribe (Chemehuevi), and Taaqtam (Serrano). These native populations did not merely glean resources from their environment; they also managed the environment to make it more hospitable. In North America, people spread plants they desired, planting crops, trees, and shrubs. Tribes such as the Cahuilla used fire to improve the productivity of palm tree groves. Aboriginal Australians such as the Gundungurra people also used fire as well as other management techniques. Modern resource managers are trying to improve their own plans by learning from traditional knowledge.

OFF-ROAD VEHICLES

For some people, nothing beats the thrill of dropping off the beaten path to ride through open land. Riders may go off-road with trucks, motorcycles, dirt bikes, snowmobiles, or all-terrain vehicles. Off-road vehicle use has skyrocketed in the American southwest since the 1960s. Unfortunately, this action is devastating large parts of the desert, including vast stretches of the California Desert Conservation Area. One pass with a vehicle is enough to start compacting the soil, which decreases its ability to absorb water. Even if drivers swerve around plants, many desert species such as the creosote bush have wide root systems the vehicle can damage. Other unseen casualties include animals crushed in burrows. Off-road vehicles have completely stripped some areas of vegetation. The Center for Biological Diversity and other conservation organizations have worked to limit off-roaders' access to sensitive locations, such as the Algodones Dunes in the Sonoran Desert.

flooding. At the same time, dams have disrupted the natural flood cycles which once shaped the riparian landscape and maintained native riparian vegetation.

DESERTIFICATION

According to the United Nations (UN), "Desertification is not the natural expansion of existing deserts but the degradation of land in arid, semiarid, and dry sub-humid areas."[2] Desertification is driven by human activities. Land becomes desert, or desert land becomes a more impoverished desert. The process has gone on for a long time. For example, parts of Jordan had lush riparian areas several centuries ago but lost them due to overgrazing.

Desertification can happen with the removal of plants and soil crusts. Without these features to hold the soil together, erosion strips away topsoil. Eroded material spreads the destruction by burying remaining plants. When people draw water from aquifers for agricultural, industrial, or residential uses, they can lower the water table. Depleting water tables may starve the environment of moisture while concentrating salt and other minerals, poisoning water sources and soils. Climate change also causes desertification by raising temperatures, which increases the rate at which water evaporates from the environment.

Desertification degrades wildlife habitat and also threatens human livelihoods. Drylands become less able to support crops or to feed livestock, and less water is available for human communities. The UN estimates 1.5 billion people are affected by land degradation, and it finds that every year drought and desertification remove the fertility of 30 million acres (12 million ha).[3] Also, desertification disproportionally affects people in lower socioeconomic classes.

Although the problem is dire, people are not helpless. Deserts and drylands can recover through hard work and proper techniques. Almost 5 billion acres (2 billion ha) worldwide have potential for restoration.[4]

MILITARY USES

So much of the desert appears empty and open, making it appealing to military planners. In the United States, for example, the military has located bases, training areas as large as cities, and even nuclear testing sites in the arid southwestern United States. Military establishments cover millions of acres in the Mojave Desert alone. Military operations and installations degrade land and damage desert vegetation, threatening animals such as desert tortoises. Large-scale maneuvers around the time of World War II (1939-1945) left tank tracks in the desert that are still visible today. Trinity Site in New Mexico, where the first atomic bomb was tested, is now a National Historic Landmark open to the public twice a year, but it still has greater levels of radiation than surrounding areas. After World War II, military buildup fueled the growth of large communities in or near the desert.

"Gazing across the desert, it is not hard to feel connected to the land and a powerful sense of something much greater. . . . We must preserve the desert for our children and grandchildren, so they may one day be able to gaze across its beauty and splendor."[5]

—*Matthew Leivas Sr., chairman of the Chemehuevi Indian Tribe and a founding board member of the Native American Land Conservancy*

Receiving national park status can help protect desert areas.

PROTECTING LAND

Cultural groups and others have set aside reserves to protect wildlife and plants for thousands of years. But when colonial and settler societies encountered deserts, they saw the areas as wasteland without inherent value, leading to a lack of regulation regarding their use.

The US Congress created Yellowstone National Park in 1872, an act that inspired countries around the world to establish national parks. Countries began seeing the importance of conserving land in a natural state, including deserts.

Preserves have varying levels of protection from human activities. The disturbances that remain depend on the preserve's designation and relevant laws. No matter what level of protection land has on paper, the actual protection it has on the ground varies.

TYPES OF PRESERVES

The International Union for Conservation of Nature recognizes several different categories of preserves, although many countries use their own designations. Deserts have different levels of protection, reflecting the fact that preserves have different goals. Strict nature preserves and wilderness have some of the highest protections, meant to strongly limit the effect of human activities. Other preserves may balance protecting an ecosystem with a variety of recreational opportunities. National parks and monuments may go this route. Some designations are meant to preserve a unique culture as well as an important ecosystem. In those cases, human harvesting of plants and animals may be an integral part of the protected area, and managers focus on ensuring the use is sustainable.

People still trespass for damaging joy rides or to poach park animals. Conservation efforts on preserves may also need to contend with threats such as invasive species and destructive roads. Despite these challenges, putting land aside is an important first step that can protect it from further degradation and can be followed later by active conservation measures. In 2003, researchers from the United Nations Environment World Conservation Monitoring Centre in England found that 14 percent of cold-winter deserts and 21 percent of warm deserts and semideserts were protected areas.[1]

THE CALIFORNIA DESERT PROTECTION ACT

In the 1800s, the US government opened up deserts in the western United States to settlers and miners without regard for the natural ecosystems. Settlers drove livestock through sensitive areas, overwhelming small watering holes and permanently changing them. In the 1920s and

President Jimmy Carter signed the Endangered American Wilderness Act of 1978. The act added approximately 1.3 million acres (530,000 ha) of wilderness in the western United States.

1930s, concern grew over the ongoing destruction in the North American deserts, and conservationists successfully pushed for the US and Mexican governments to protect large stretches. In 1964, protections on some US public lands increased when the government

"These desert wildlands display unique scenic, historical, archeological, environmental, ecological, wildlife, cultural, scientific, educational, and recreational values used and enjoyed by millions of Americans for hiking and camping, scientific study and scenic appreciation."[4]

—Text from the California Desert Protection Act of 1994

THE WILDERNESS ACT

Recognizing the value of leaving portions of land in a wild state, US Congress passed the Wilderness Act in 1964. In the United States, wilderness is the category of land with the highest level of protection. While humans can still visit wilderness lands, the law bans permanent living or other signs of human activity. With some exceptions, the act excluded motorized vehicles and roads, even temporary ones. The Wilderness Act immediately designated more than 9 million acres (3.7 million ha) of wilderness land. By 2014, the amount of wilderness in the United States increased to almost 110 million acres (44.5 million ha).[5]

passed the Wilderness Act, creating wilderness as the strictest category of protection. Wilderness is meant to stay permanently wild, free of human activities or buildings and driven by natural processes.

Three decades later, in 1994, the US government made another large commitment to desert conservation when the California Desert Protection Act finally passed after years of work and political maneuvering. The law created more wilderness in the lower 48 states than any act since the Wilderness Act, totaling almost 7.6 million acres (3 million ha) total.[2]

The law upgraded Death Valley and Joshua Tree National Monument into national parks and expanded the land they covered. It created the Mojave National Preserve and 69 new wilderness areas, placed under the management of the Bureau of Land Management (BLM).[3] This new land had a purpose: bridge the gap between the national parks. Connections between conservation areas allow wildlife to move between them, keeping populations from becoming isolated. In its own right, the new land also protected habitat for thousands of desert species, including Joshua trees and desert tortoises.

Repeated attempts to pass an updated California Protection Act that would create even more links between reserves failed, so conservationists turned to the president rather than Congress. In 2016, President Barack Obama heeded their advice and designated three new national monuments for a total of 1.8 million acres (0.7 million ha).[6] These preserves are the Mojave Trails National Monument, Sand to Snow National Monument, and Castle Mountains National Monument.

In 2017, President Donald Trump signed an executive order calling for a review of national monuments designated since 1996 with the aim of shrinking or eliminating some, putting the future of these desert preserves in jeopardy. However, local support for the areas and the recreational activities they provide may still protect them.

BUREAU OF LAND MANAGEMENT

Now a manager of wilderness as well as exploited landscapes, the BLM has its origin back in the days when the West was up for sale. In 1812, the United States created the General Land Office to encourage settlement on land acquired by the government. In 1934, the US Grazing Service began, and in 1946 the government combined the two agencies to create the BLM. Except in wilderness and explicit conservation areas, BLM land is not intended to be preserved solely for its natural character. It is managed for multiple human uses including grazing, mining, and, in the foreseeable future, solar energy production.

"We've been successful in Namibia because we dreamed of a future that was much more than just a healthy wildlife. We knew conservation would fail if it doesn't work to improve the lives of the local communities."[7]

—John Kasaona, director of the Integrated Rural Development and Nature Conservation in Namibia

DESERT CHEETAHS

The fastest land animal, the cheetah, is rapidly disappearing, with only 7,100 remaining in 2016.[10] The number of cheetahs worldwide has been cut in half since 1975. Desert cheetahs in particular are in trouble. Cheetahs in the Sahara have lost 91 percent of their range.[11] The population in Iran contains fewer than 50 of these animals.[12] Desert cheetahs roam over a large area and are relatively shy, complicating efforts to study their vulnerable populations. Scientists find it difficult to determine basic information about the cats' population numbers and habitat use. Scientists must use innovative techniques to monitor them, such as scat analysis and camera traps. Genetic tests can identify individuals by their scat, while cameras take advantage of the fact that each cheetah sports a unique pattern of spots.

OTHER PROTECTED AREAS WORLDWIDE

Namibia, a country in Southern Africa that is home to the Namib Desert, has been a huge conservation success story, with 17 percent of its land belonging to a network of protected areas.[8] In addition to state-run parks, local communities have set up many special conservation areas of their own. Protections have led to huge increases in mammal populations such as oryx, lions, and cheetahs, while conservation and tourism provide jobs for local people.

Governments and communities continue to set aside desert lands and dry lands. In 2012, Niger, a country in West Africa, created the Termit and Tin Toumma National Nature Reserve as 37,452 square miles (97,000 sq km) of protected desert lands in the Sahara, making it one of the largest areas of protected land in Africa.[9] Wildlife within the reserve include critically endangered species such as the dama gazelle and the Saharan cheetah.

The Sahara Desert covers most of North Africa, including large sections of Chad, Egypt, Algeria, Mali, and Libya.

Red brome is one invasive species that still plagues the Mojave Desert.

TACKLING INVASIVE SPECIES

P lants and animals have always wandered from the locations where they
evolved, but with the rise of human travel across oceans and through the air,
species have moved farther and faster than ever before. Many non-natives that
people bring to a new area never escape cultivation. But others thrive, having
left behind the predators, competitors, and diseases that kept their numbers in
check back home. When these successful non-natives cause harm to their new
environment, or are expected to cause harm, they are called invasive species.

Harsh conditions keep many non-native species out of the desert, but not all.
About 5 percent of plants in the Mojave Desert are non-native.[1] The problem is

worse in riparian habitats because water is more available. People brought some invaders on purpose, hoping to use them for agriculture, landscaping, or to prevent erosion.

For example, people attempted to rehabilitate degraded lands in North America by planting African lovegrass, which then became invasive. Other times, the introduction and spread of invasive species are accidental as species hitch a ride on vehicles or animals or take up residence in areas disturbed by construction.

Invasive plants in deserts cause problems by not only competing with native plants for scarce resources, but also changing the environment and altering ecological processes. Tamarisk, an invasive species in Australia, Africa, and North America, lowers the water table and deposits salt in the soil. Several invading grasses support wildfires that native plants are not equipped to survive. In general, invasive species provide less value to other wildlife than the natives they replace. Sometimes a native species such as desert broom, a shrub, responds to human activities by expanding its population and causing environmental harm.

Conservation of native landscapes requires control of invasive species. Many invaders prefer disturbed areas, so a degraded desert left to recover on its own may instead transform into an alien landscape. Managers have successfully handled invasive species in some desert lands using multiple techniques.

UPROOTING INVADERS

Land managers may eliminate invasive plants by cutting or uprooting them. Herbicides are a powerful weapon in a conservationist's arsenal, although they must be used carefully. People can directly apply herbicides to the cut stems of desert invaders such as giant reed or Russian olive to keep them from growing back, or they may spray herbicides when other options are too difficult because the patch is too large or inaccessible. In riparian areas, managers can use floods to disrupt dense patches of invasive tamarisk.

INVASIVE QUALITIES

Of all the plants and animals moved around the world by humans, only a fraction will cause extensive problems. Unfortunately, managers can't identify problem species ahead of time. Often, a new species spreads slowly for decades before exploding across the landscape. But some factors do make a species more likely to invade. Invasive species are often generalists, which means they are not confined to a narrow set of conditions, helping them aggressively compete for resources. Most invaders reproduce and grow quickly, allowing them to rapidly colonize an area.

Physical management requires a lot of time and effort. Infested areas will need to be cleared multiple times as some plants recover and new seeds germinate. Still, with a strong commitment, physical control can be extremely effective, especially for small areas or new infestations.

Buffelgrass is causing huge problems in the deserts of North America and Australia. People brought buffelgrass from Eurasia and Africa in the 1900s to feed livestock. After a slow start, buffelgrass populations exploded, especially along roadways. Buffelgrass not only crowds out other plants, but also fuels hot fires that kill native plants. Buffelgrass is best controlled by a combination of pulling, grazing, and herbicides. Concentrated effort

Buffelgrass kills native plants by stealing their water resources and increasing fire risk in desert areas.

has effectively removed buffelgrass from protected areas such as JTNP, Saguaro National Park, and Organ Pipe National Monument.

Managers have also successfully controlled other invaders in the preserves of the American Southwest. In 2010, Saguaro National Park reported having eradicated problem species such as giant cane, common oat, cheatgrass, watermelon, African daisy, flax, cheeseweed, tree tobacco, and two species of non-native prickly pears. Other invasive species were still present.

BIOLOGICAL CONTROL

Biological control is the management of an unwanted species using a living agent such as lady beetles, which are the predators of crop-eating aphids. When managers introduce non-natives for the purpose of controlling invasive species, they must take precautions. Otherwise the control agent could become an invasive species in its own right. Agents are tested to make sure they don't target native species,

FIERY GRASSES

Despite being dry, most deserts don't burn well. There's not enough organic matter to act as fuel. Even if one plant catches on fire, the flames typically won't spread. Unfortunately, invasive grasses like red brome, cheatgrass, and buffelgrass change the equation. They fill in the spaces between desert plants and, during dry periods, act as torches to turn a spark into an inferno. Native species in the Mojave and Sonoran Deserts have not evolved strategies to survive wildfires, while the roots of invasive grasses survive a blaze. These hot fires encourage the growth of these non-native grasses.

for example. To be successful, agents must also reproduce rapidly enough to suppress their prey.

Testing a biological agent is expensive and time-consuming. However, once the initial work concludes, the organism might form a self-sustaining population in the wild. It can continue to work without much help. For invasive species established over millions of acres, biological control gives managers a powerful tool to restore balance to an out-of-control non-native.

In the 1800s, Europeans released rabbits into the wilds of Australia as game for hunting. Billions of rabbits spread far and wide, adapting well to deserts and other Australian habitats. The rabbits devoured native vegetation, even creating new desert lands. Native plant populations crashed. Not only did animals have to compete with the appetites of the invaders, but they were also eaten by increasing populations of invasive predators such as feral cats

Rabbits impacted the desert biodiversity in Australia.

THE HISTORY OF BIOLOGICAL CONTROL

Attempts at biological control in the past have ended with the newcomer wreaking havoc. Asian lady beetles, released in the 1970s to control aphid pests in the southeastern United States, have spread widely and threaten native ladybug populations. Weevils released around the same time to control non-native thistles are now driving North American thistles toward extinction. Even with the strictest precautions, accidents can happen, such as the one that released rabbit hemorrhagic disease before scientists were ready. And once released, a control species might affect ecosystems in unexpected ways. Scientists must always weigh the dangers against the potential benefits.

and foxes that thrived on a bunny diet. The double punch of competition and predation drove some native species to extinction.

People tried to contain the destruction of habitat by erecting miles of rabbit fences and by destroying rabbit burrows. In 1950, scientists turned to a biological control agent, the Myxoma virus. Although the virus had high success rates at first, it required mosquitoes to spread, and therefore did not work very well in arid regions. As rabbits grew resistant to the Myxoma virus, scientists began testing other disease agents such as rabbit hemorrhagic disease.

In 1995, before experiments could finish on a nearby island, flies snuck rabbit hemorrhagic disease to mainland Australia. For once, a biological control accident turned out well. The virus raced through the rabbit populations of Australia, reaching into desert areas. Vegetation and large native herbivores like kangaroos began to recover. Twenty years later, scientists discovered that vulnerable desert populations of dusky hopping mice, plains mice, and

Settlers from Europe brought the fox to Australia in the 1850s for sporting purposes.

ENVIRONMENTAL CONTEXT MATTERS

A species that solves problems in one place may cause them in another. For example, Cactoblastis moths once took part in one of the biggest conservation success stories in history: the control of prickly pear cacti in Australia. People first introduced prickly pears for agriculture. Prickly pear cacti species spread rapidly, infesting millions of acres of forest and grasslands by the 1900s. In the 1920s, scientists fought back by releasing various insects, including a Cactoblastis moth. The strategy paid off, and the insects drastically reduced prickly pear populations, although they didn't work well in the driest conditions. Now, though, Cactoblastis moths have spread into Florida. Managers fear they will jump to the deserts of North America, where native prickly pears feed both wildlife and humans. Fortunately, the Cactoblastis moth may not be able to survive the desert.

the crest-tailed mulgara had drastically increased. Trapping surveys showed that their rise coincided with that of the new virus.

Biological control has been successful against invasive desert plants as well. Puncturevine, which arrived in American deserts in the early 1900s, was reduced to low levels by the puncturevine seed weevil that was released beginning in the 1970s. While manual and chemical controls have been effective against tamarisk in managed areas like JTNP, infestations were out of control in other areas. Scientists added another tool to their arsenal by identifying a group of effective biological control agents: tamarisk leaf beetles. Scientists released four beetle species beginning in 2001, starting with 10 sites throughout six western states.[3]

The insect spread and defoliated tamarisks so successfully that biologists became worried about the southwestern willow flycatcher, an endangered native song bird that nests extensively in tamarisk. Fortunately, by 2010 many flycatchers had shifted back to nesting in native willows.

When large numbers of invasive species like the tamarisk die, it frees up land for new invasive species. Conservationists often must combine biological control with other management actions in order to restore native species or ecological functions.

SIGNS OF HOPE

While invasive species have been eradicated or controlled over some large areas, they still infest many others. Many invaders are here to stay. Eventually, native predators might evolve to eat them and native species might evolve to successfully compete with them, although management may be necessary in the short term to ensure native species survive long enough. In the Mojave Desert, people have established cooperative weed management areas in which managers determine the non-natives within their region and prioritize which species to control based on the level of threat they pose.

Scientists are also watching for new problems. When a species is a recognized threat, managers can monitor for new, small infestations and act before the population becomes too large to manage. Conservationists educate the public about the dangers of planting non-native species known to cause problems. Governments restrict or prohibit certain invasive plants to keep them from spreading to new areas. With hard work, public education, and monitoring, land managers can continue to push back against non-native species invading the deserts of the world.

The California condor population grew after conservationists found ways to help the birds return to their native environment.

RETURNING DESERT BIODIVERSITY

Unregulated hunting, habitat loss, overgrazing, invasive species, pollution, and vehicle traffic are some things that threaten the biodiversity of deserts. Biodiversity refers to variation among living things, both the variety of different species and the genetic variation within a species. A related term, richness, means the number of different species present in an area. Losing biodiversity is not just about losing individual species. When species lose genetic diversity, they lose the raw material needed to evolve to meet changing conditions. And when one species is lost, it may affect many others since desert organisms often form complex food webs with each other. For example, grasshopper mice in southern California eat a variety of prey such as arthropods and arthropod-eating lizards, while the mice are themselves eaten by predators such as coyotes and raptors.

"Biologists have long seen deserts as laboratories of nature, where natural selection is exposed at its most extreme."[3]
—David Ward, author of The Biology of Deserts

Deserts are surprisingly diverse. Twelve percent of the world's biodiversity hotspots are found in desert lands.[1] Many scientists consider the harshness of the desert an excellent driver of evolution, leading to many unique adaptations. For example, as of 2016 the Succulent Karoo in Africa, a particularly diverse desert, harbored 4,850 different plant species, of which 1,490 were endemic.[2]

Although human actions have threatened biodiversity around the world, some people have worked hard to turn the tide. Native biodiversity benefits when people protect land and manage invasive species, but some species also require direct interventions. Conservationists have rescued populations in dire straits, such as the Arabian oryx, and they have worked to address threats before they could drive species like desert bighorns toward extinction.

RESURRECTING LOST SPECIES

Species have always gone extinct, but because of the environmental changes caused by human activity, the rate of species loss has skyrocketed in recent times. Extinction in the wild usually lasts forever, but not always. Some species have gone extinct in the wild only to be returned after years of captive breeding. These include several animals that either live in the desert, such as the Arabian oryx, or use desert habitat, such as the California condor.

The Arabian oryx is a medium-sized antelope in the Arabian Desert, located northeast of Africa. Hunting pushed the species to extinction in the wild by the 1970s. Fortunately, the oryx survived in captive herds in zoos. Conservationists and others began a captive breeding program. Ten captive-bred oryx were released into Oman, a country on the Arabian Peninsula, in 1982 after a decade without wild Arabian oryx. The program expanded with reintroductions into Israel, Saudi Arabia, the United Arab Emirates, and Jordan. In 2011, with approximately 1,000 oryx in the

DESIGNING PRESERVES FOR BIODIVERSITY

When preserved land is meant to protect biodiversity, the design of the preserve itself influences how well it performs this function. Sometimes the most effective way to conserve many species is by protecting the habitat for one wide-ranging species, such as desert-dwelling elephants. Presumably, by protecting an area large enough to house elephants, a preserve would catch a higher biodiversity within its boundaries compared with a smaller protected area. Biodiversity includes genetic variation within a species as well as a diversity of species. Small, isolated populations are more likely to lose unique genes than larger populations that breed with each other. To keep gene flow, conservationists must also consider protecting corridors for travel between protected areas.

INTERNATIONAL STATUS

The International Union for Conservation of Nature (IUCN) Red List is a list of the conservation statuses of species worldwide. Species in the most desperate situations are categorized as critically endangered, endangered, or vulnerable. Species whose populations are more secure may be assessed as near threatened or least concern. Although the IUCN listings are not enforceable, they guide global conservation efforts. Having legal protections can be enormously effective. The majority of species listed in the United States under the Endangered Species Act, which protects threatened and endangered species, have so far avoided extinction.

wild, the population had recovered enough for the IUCN Red List to upgrade the species' classification to vulnerable, 41 years after the oryx had gone extinct.[4]

California condors are the largest raptors in North America. Condors are strictly scavengers and once foraged for carcasses throughout the southwestern United States, frequenting the coasts and deserts. Condor numbers plummeted as they clashed with humans. People shot them and collected their eggs. Many condors died by colliding with power lines or were poisoned by cyanide in coyote traps or lead ammunition in carcasses.

Fortunately, conservationists realized the condor was in trouble. The Peregrine Fund, which aims to save raptors from extinction, created a condor breeding program. A team of biologists captured the last wild California condor in 1987, although the Andean condor persisted in South America. Five years later, the Peregrine Fund began releases in Arizona, and the California condor once again flew freely in North America. By 2016, the wild population had increased to 276 birds.[5]

Arabian oryx can weigh up to 200 pounds (90 kg).

ENGINEERING A RELEASE

Captive-bred animals pose problems for managers looking to release them. They may not know how to survive in the wild. Many captive condors did not even have bird parents to teach them to hunt or avoid dangers. To increase the rate of condor reproduction, caretakers in zoos like the Los Angeles Zoo removed one egg from a condor pair each year to raise by hand. To avoid the birds imprinting on humans, keepers used puppets made to look like condor parents. Unfortunately, these hand-raised birds did not get the same socialization as condor-raised birds. Caretakers began allowing young birds to spend time with adult condors before release. Once the birds fly free, biologists help support them with medicine and food as they learn to live on their own.

When the Syrian wild ass disappeared in the wild in the early 1900s because of over-hunting, scientists had no captive animals left to work with. The Syrian wild ass was truly extinct. The Syrian wild ass was a subspecies of the Asiatic wild ass, a horse relative that still existed in both captive and wild herds, although these populations also faced dire threats. Beginning in 1982, biologists bred other subspecies in captivity until they had enough animals to release into the empty ranges of the Syrian wild ass. Approximately 250 wild asses roamed the Negev Desert by 2016.[6]

Desert bighorn sheep were headed the way of the Arabian oryx and Syrian wild ass before managers intervened. The desert bighorn is a subspecies of bighorn sheep adapted to survive in the arid mountains of the southwestern United States. Hunting and habitat loss reduced bighorn sheep from hundreds of thousands of animals to only about 15,000 by the early 1900s.[7]

Thanks to conservationists, bighorns did not become extinct in the wild. New national parks meant some bighorn herds gained legal protections. Government agencies trapped individuals from stable herds and released them in places without surviving bighorn herds. People also bred and released captive bighorns to boost wild numbers. Bighorn

Desert bighorn sheep rams'
curled horns grow throughout
their lives.

populations have recovered, although they still face threats. Livestock compete with bighorns for food, but domestic herds also present a different problem: disease. Contact between wild and domesticated animals can spread dangerous respiratory illnesses. In some areas, people work to prohibit livestock grazing to protect bighorns.

PROTECTING VULNERABLE SPECIES

In the United States, the Endangered Species Act protects species that are determined to be endangered or threatened with extinction. The act also requires the US Fish and Wildlife Service to develop recovery plans for endangered species. Conserving one species may require protecting its habitat, an action that will benefit all the other species that rely on the same habitat.

The US government placed the southwestern willow flycatcher on the endangered species list in 1995 because of declines related to habitat loss. The flycatchers breed in riparian areas in North America, then spend the winter in Central America. Recovery efforts to restore suitable riparian habitat have led to slow gains in the willow flycatcher population. For example, in 2008, biologists monitoring the willow flycatcher found only eight breeding pairs in Washington County, Utah, but they found 13 successful nests in 2014 after restoration work had been done.[8] Private landowners have helped flycatchers by restoring thousands of acres of riparian areas through the Working Lands for Wildlife partnership run by the US Department of Agriculture.

Two species of desert tortoise live in the Mojave and Sonoran Deserts, spending much of their long lives underground. That hasn't saved them from human changes to their deserts. Development, overgrazing, vehicles, disease, and the collection of individual tortoises by people has greatly reduced their populations. Because of this, the Mojave Desert tortoise is listed as threatened.

> "Tortoises are so long lived, living up to 100 years we think, so some of the positive results of what we are doing may not be seen for a while."[9]
>
> —Brian J. Wooldridge, a US Fish and Wildlife Service biologist, on conservation of the desert tortoise

Management plans and laws protect the species, and conservationists have worked to limit off-road vehicles and grazing in tortoise habitats. These limitations on human uses of desert lands benefit many other organisms. The tortoises themselves make burrows that often provide homes for other desert animals. Burrows can also help oxygen and water reach deeper into the soil.

One species is particularly well known for its effect on the environment: the beaver. By building dams and controlling water flow, beavers expand and improve riparian habitats to the benefit of other desert species. Although the beaver is not listed as endangered or threatened, hunting and trapping in the past removed the animals from their vital role in the southwestern United States. Their loss destabilized streams and disrupted nutrient cycles. Now scientists are restoring them to places including the San Pedro River in Arizona and Sonora, Mexico, where they have been associated with increases in bird biodiversity and water flow.

Cougars are also called pumas or mountain lions.

HOPE FOR THE FUTURE

Although some desert species have been brought back from the brink of extinction, their future still requires active management and oversight. Poaching drove one population of restored Arabian oryx into local extinction. Wild California condors must still be periodically treated for buildups of lead from ammunition or else the population could crash once again. But with continued conservation work, animals like these will continue to roam desert lands.

Some animals are even recovering on their own, although some bring their own challenges. In North America, cougars and black bears are recolonizing parts of their former range, including desert lands. As these large predators move into areas no longer used to their presence, they can come into conflict with humans and domesticated animals. Cougars even put pressure on vulnerable populations of desert bighorn. Proper management and public education can help keep the peace.

For some native animals, development has created opportunities as well as threats. Suburban areas contain excess water, gardens, and other sources of food. Because of this bounty, quail, mourning doves, packrats, and cottontail rabbit populations have been found to be higher in desert suburbs than in the open desert lands of the American Southwest.

RAVENS RUN AMOK

In the southwestern United States, ravens benefit from human activities. They exploit irrigation water. They're resourceful in finding food in human-dominated areas, foraging in trash cans, landfills, and along the side of the road for roadkill. The proliferation of power lines gives ravens more places to nest as well as to perch while looking for food. Unfortunately, increased populations of these predators put more pressure on other native species. Most significantly, ravens kill young desert tortoises. Conservationists have spread the word for people to secure their trash and avoid creating water sources such as artificial ponds.

When riparian habitats are restored, biodiversity is protected and natural resources are enhanced.

RESTORING DESERT LANDS

Human activity in the desert has left a legacy of degraded lands, from areas cleared by overgrazing to mining pits where the very ground has been stripped away to reach the minerals underneath. Sometimes people have a chance to restore these altered ecosystems. Managers of parks and reserves are limited by their budget, human resources, and time. Other restoration projects may be done by environmentalists, community groups, or collaborations of people interested in the desert ecosystem.

Deserts are slow to recover on their own because of scarce resources, challenging conditions, and the slow growth of many desert plants. Some changes

RESTORATION ECOLOGY

Restoration ecology is the branch of ecosystem study that deals with the science of returning degraded land to a more natural state through biological and physical interventions. The benefit of restoring such land may be obvious, but the benefit of studying restoration is that ecology is rarely straightforward. For example, people have found that seeds planted in the desert and watered by sprinkle irrigation tend to fail. Herbivores may concentrate on eating them if the rest of the desert is dry and dormant. By studying these and other problems, scientists can develop more effective ways to restore biodiversity and healthy ecosystems.

over the last couple of hundred years are permanent: animals have gone extinct, many non-native plants can only be controlled rather than eradicated, and indigenous residents have been removed from deserts they used and managed in the past. But improvement is possible. Through research, hard work, and trial and error, conservationists have developed methods for returning native plants and ecological systems to devastated lands.

RECLAIMING LAND

The ultimate conservation goal for restoration is returning ecological functions to degraded land, not just adding vegetation. Ecosystem functions, also called ecological processes, are all the biological, chemical, and physical processes that happen within an ecosystem. These processes drive the cycle of nutrients and water and make habitats for organisms. When natural functions return to a site, the environment itself can help protect and improve the health of the desert.

An ideal restoration plan includes several steps. After identifying a site, managers consider the landscape in which the land functions. For example, they might look at what type of land surrounds the site, how water moves through the area, conditions at the site itself, and priorities for conservation or restoration. Managers can stop active disturbance by closing roads and putting up barriers. Restoration plans should address any present invasive species, because aggressive invaders might outcompete natives in a recovering ecosystem. Even after an initial treatment, invasive species may lurk in the soil, waiting to germinate.

Both wind and water heavily erode areas that have lost vegetation and soil crusts. Flooding may carve out ditches and gullies, the presence of which contributes to even more flooding during the next rain event. Flooding washes away soil, seeds, and vegetation. It's easier to prevent big gullies from forming than to fill them in once they've formed. Managers can sculpt the landscape and add barriers such as fences and dams to control water flow and erosion. Water retention helps speed desert recovery by promoting plant growth. People sometimes make many small pits in the ground to catch water, seeds, and soil organisms.

ROADS AND TRAILS

Roads create one advantage during restoration: desert natives can more easily colonize a thin strip of cleared land than a large square. The surrounding desert is closer to the bare soil, making it so that seeds and spores don't have to travel as far. But roads bring other challenges. Traffic destroys soil crusts and compacts the ground. Even when dirt roads are closed, people don't always stay off once a passage has been established, and off-roaders are especially drawn to obvious trails. Land managers therefore can focus on restoring and hiding intersections. Vertical mulching, rock mulching, and plantings can camouflage the turn.

Conservationists germinate cottonwoods to plant in riparian habitats.

Native plants are more than something pretty to look at. They sculpt the environment around them, catching resources such as soil from passing wind or water. Plants provide important habitats for native animals. Native plants can be salvaged from construction sites where the desert will be cleared. Salvage saves individual plants from destruction and helps revegetate a restoration site. Transplanting can be expensive, but it can quickly create dramatic results.

Nurseries can also nurture seeds until the plants have grown large enough to survive the desert environment. Whether it uses seeds, seedlings, or adult plants, a planting project must provide enough water for plants to become established. Irrigating remote sites is difficult and expensive, but conservationists have developed some techniques to address this problem. Some restoration plans rely only on catching rainwater. Other plans call for irrigation systems or adding artificial material to the soil that absorbs and releases moisture.

Managers can provide a focus for the desert to heal itself further by creating resource islands. In intact deserts, soil fertility is higher underneath shrubs. A restoration project near Los Angeles around 1970 had generally low success with native plantings. However, shrubs growing on hills had formed islands of native vegetation two decades later. Shrub roots dig into the soil, holding it together and allowing water to seep underground more easily. The trunk and canopy of the desert shrub break the wind and catch soil as it floats or blows by. Seeds are caught, too, and can take advantage of the shade and moisture provided by the shrub, as can desert animals.

People have developed many ways to support plantings or help the desert heal itself. In China,

REVIVING SOILS

Soil characteristics affect the success of a restoration project. Living crusts and other soil microorganisms are hard to rehabilitate, although erosion control can help the land trap microorganisms and soil needed for them to grow on. Managers have also developed techniques for adding microorganisms to the soil or, more effectively, to plant roots with which they form symbiotic relationships. Living soil crusts can be removed from salvage sites and spread on restoration land. Restoration projects can also use salvaged topsoil, which adds organic matter to a site.

managers have used windbreaks for decades to protect plantings of native shrubs in deserts, successfully revegetating areas along many railways. One study in the Tengger Desert found healthy living soil crusts four decades later.

Similar to shrubs and trees, vertical mulching can catch soil and seeds while increasing water infiltration into the ground. Conservationists have also used dead stalks to create nesting habitats for native bees, as well as specifically planting flowers to nurture the many pollinators that live in the desert.

RECLAIMING RIPARIAN AREAS

Healthy riparian areas are important resources for plants and animals in desert ecosystems. The lush, dense vegetation provides an ample cover and breeding habitat for animals such as nesting birds. In the Mojave Desert, riparian habitats are home to several federally listed species such as the arroyo toad and the Mohave tui chub, a type of fish. Restoring these ecosystems can greatly benefit native biodiversity.

Restored riparian areas perform ecological functions other than just providing habitat. They clean water by filtering it, decrease erosion, and absorb damaging flood waters. Riparian habitats have suffered disproportionally from human activity, but moist riparian conditions also make restoration easier and faster than in the open desert. Water can be a challenge as well as an opportunity, since desert floods can destroy restoration plantings.

Lee Vining Creek flows into Mono Lake.

Since humans have drastically altered the flow of water into and through riparian areas, restoring water flow can begin the recovery of many sites. In Lee Vining Creek in the Great Basin Desert in California, a lawsuit returned water to the creek, which had been diverted for water and power generation by the city of Los Angeles. The return of water supported restoration plantings.

Managers can manipulate water levels to perform ecological functions. Managers in the Owen's River watershed in California used multiple floods to establish native plants. One flood prepared the streamside soil, followed by more flooding to spread native seeds and trigger them to germinate. Riparian areas can also start recovering on their own when livestock are removed from an area or at least fenced away from the water.

When given free access to streams and springs, livestock prefer to spend their time in and around them. They destabilize streams and inhibit plant recovery. After grazing pressure is eased, a muddy streak through the landscape becomes a green ribbon. A study led by a researcher from the Natural History Museum of Utah examined an enclosed riparian area in semiarid land in the Great Basin over a span of 50 years. Compared with nearby grazed land, the protected area had greater diversity of both plants and small mammals. Even restricting grazing of the riparian areas to the early spring can have dramatic results on plant recovery.

Just as in the open desert, effective restoration programs in riparian areas usually involve a mix of techniques. People must manage invasive plants such as tamarisk, giant reed, and Russian olive. Managers use manual control and herbicides, but sometimes carefully controlled grazing or fire can help.

While mature riparian plants inhibit erosion, erosion may damage or remove plants that are trying to establish themselves. By reshaping the land and adding dams, people can start the process of erosion control. Additionally, riparian plantings in the American Southwest may need protection from livestock, elk, or beaver.

Riparian restoration can produce impressive results. In 2012, the Mexican and US governments made an agreement allowing some of the water diverted for the use of farms and cities to instead flow to parts of the Colorado River Delta. Within months, trees planted in one 250-acre (100-ha) plot had grown taller than a person and had already attracted migratory birds and native predators.[2]

RESTORING THE DESERT

More desert areas need restoration, which is not always a priority. For one thing, people don't always grasp the potential deserts have for improvement. Government agents in the United States rehabilitated riparian areas and then brought ranchers to see the results. The ranchers were amazed at the lushness that was possible compared to the barren landscapes they were used to.

POLE CUTTINGS

People can grow trees and shrubs in nurseries before transferring them, roots and all, to a restoration site. But for some fast-growing trees, including cottonwoods and willows, using pole cuttings produces better results. In the middle of winter, when trees are dormant, people harvest poles and remove all but the top two branches. When hydrated and then placed in the ground near a source of water, the poles will form new roots and leaves.

More and more people are beginning to understand the importance of ecological functions such as water control and pollination of plants, including human crops. Legions of volunteers and staff at preserves and nonprofits work hard on plantings and controlling invasive species over large areas. With education, perhaps more people will join in, and rehabilitation and restoration can spread to more desert areas that need help.

People across the globe live and thrive in desert environments.

EIGHT

SUSTAINING USE

Throughout the world, people depend on deserts. According to the United Nations, about one-third of the world's population live in drylands, with 5.8 percent in deserts and semideserts.[1] These people aren't going away. Although full recovery is hampered when humans are still using an area, that doesn't mean the deserts are lost to conservation. Humans can manage their use of water, soil, and other natural resources to reduce waste, and modern agriculture can learn from the ecological resource management of traditional and ancient cultures.

Landowners can be powerful allies in conservation work. Desertification harms human communities as well as natural ones. The health of an ecosystem affects the fertility of its soil and the productivity of the native plant community.

AGROFORESTRY

Agroforestry is a system that combines human food production with woody plants, which may include shrubs. Agroforestry doesn't just mean a pasture with trees. The farmer or rancher must intentionally plan and manage both the agricultural and the forestry aspects. Examples of arid agroforestry systems include olive trees interplanted with grain crops in the Negev Desert in Israel or goats carefully pastured with mesquite trees in the Thar Desert of India. Restoring riparian areas within agricultural lands is a form of agroforestry if it returns riparian trees to areas where livestock graze or crops are grown. Agroforestry can fight against desertification, protect natural resources, and provide a habitat for wildlife.

Just as the natural world can assist humans, human activities can be structured to aid biodiversity. Well-managed grazing preserves room for wildlife habitat, and agroforestry techniques can guard against destructive erosion. Agricultural scientists are looking for other ways in which farming can use fewer resources and cause less damage to surrounding environments.

WORKING WITH LOCALS

Conservation is costly, and government budgets are limited. By turning to local communities' traditional ecological knowledge, conservation efforts can take advantage of the people already living and working in a habitat. Some programs deploy staff to provide training, expertise, and equipment while letting local people spread the tools through their community. Farmers can teach and support each other with more credibility than outsiders can.

Landcare in Australia has followed this model of community conservation. Using a limited amount of government funding, the program empowers local leaders to pursue restoration goals. People have formed more than 4,000 locally based groups, with more than 40 percent of Australian farmers involved.[2] Farmers and ranchers also have access to an informational service run by Greening Australia. They've used their training to support native plants and manage other resources on their own properties, reaching far more acres than the government could by focusing only on public lands.

Invasive species cause huge damage to cropland and livestock as well as to native species, making farmers and conservationists natural allies in management efforts. The challenge increases, though, when a conservation goal appears to oppose the interests of landowners. Although harder, the goal is not impossible. For example, in the Karoo, a desert in South Africa, sheep farmers have a history of dealing with native predators by killing them. Sheep farmers in the Karoo can be hit hard by predators, especially by black-backed jackals, generalist predators and

THE BENEFITS OF HEALTHY ECOSYSTEMS

When human land uses are modified to benefit biodiversity, it also benefits human communities. Functioning landscapes can help control floods, while healthy predator populations may help manage agricultural pests. Without the pollinator services provided by the environment, many crops would struggle to produce fruit and seeds. Less tangibly, healthy deserts can provide human visitors with opportunities for recreation and reflection.

"Established pest animals and weeds are problems that simply will not go away. A new approach to how they are collectively managed is needed. Empowering those impacted by the pests to take action is the key to success."[3]

—Andrew Woolnough, from the State Government of Victoria in Australia

Black-backed jackals live in various habitats, including woodland savannahs and coastal deserts.

scavengers who eat anything from insects to beached marine mammals.

Farmers in the Karoo are becoming more open to nonlethal methods of controlling predation. Many are interested in protecting biodiversity as well as sheep, while recognizing that jackals will never be exterminated completely and that lethal control can sometimes increase the loss of sheep, perhaps by increasing jackal reproduction. To develop the science to better address conflicts between farmers and predators, researchers have teamed up with sheep herders for the Karoo Predator Project. Farmers help live-trap predators on their own land for study. Researchers can learn more about the movement and diets of native predators while farmers have a chance to form a different relationship with these creatures.

DESERT GARDENING

People living in arid landscapes can garden with thirsty species that require irrigation, yet people are increasingly choosing desert plants. Desert species require less watering, leaving more for natural environments. While non-natives can work, native desert plants are already adapted to the local environment and pollinators and pose less threat of becoming invasive. Small gardens provide limited ecosystem functions compared with large restoration sites, but they may create habitat for native wildlife. Native flowers can provide nectar and pollen for pollinators. Gardeners should look for nursery-grown plants rather than plants removed from the desert.

One challenge for desert conservation is urban development.

THE FUTURE DESERT

The future of deserts around the world depends on the actions of landowners and public or protected land managers, as well as larger global trends in areas such as development and the climate. In some places, people have made great progress against threats such as invasive species and biodiversity losses. Some invaders have been removed from areas as large as JTNP, and animals including the Arabian oryx have been snatched from the edge of extinction.

Many challenges remain. Invasive plants still infest huge areas. Researchers are working on new techniques to help fight them. The expanding thirst of civilization is putting pressure on natural water sources and leading to water stress in cities and

Solar and wind power are renewable energy resources.

conflicts between countries. Development, including the creation of large windmill and solar power installations, is gobbling up desert land.

In addition, one enormous threat is looming over habitats all around the world: climate change. Human activities, such as creating landfills and burning fossil fuels, pump excess greenhouse gases into the atmosphere. There, the gases trap increasing amounts of heat and cause the planet to warm. Deserts are among the most vulnerable ecosystems to shifts in the climate because of their extreme conditions. Desert organisms often live on the edge, making do with scarce resources that are easily disrupted.

RENEWABLE ENERGY IN THE DESERT

The fight against climate change has led to a push for renewable energy projects. Deserts have always attracted people with their large and seemingly empty spaces, and the abundance of sun and wind have been particularly appealing. While renewable energy is often described as green energy, a large solar installation still represents industrial development. It destroys habitat, uses desert resources, brings roads, pollutes, and kills animals directly. In 2016, the Desert Renewable Energy Conservation Plan protected 9.2 million acres (3.7 million ha) of federal land from solar, wind, or geothermal development. It left 800,000 acres (323,749 ha) open to projects on land deemed less ecologically valuable.[2]

A CHANGING CLIMATE

Earth's climate is never static. During the last Ice Age, which ended 11,500 years ago, the planet looked very different than it does now.[1] Cold deserts covered vast stretches of North America and Europe, while some areas that supported woodlands at the time are now covered with deserts. After the Ice Age ended, massive changes took place in the world's climate, leading to a more current-looking globe.

"GREEN SAHARA"

In the desolate Sahara Desert, hunter-gatherers once created vibrant images in caves and under rock outcrops. The pictures, created from 11,000 to 5,000 years ago during the last African Humid Period, depict herds of large mammals such as elephants and antelopes, which lived in the "Green Sahara."[3] Climate change brought both the beginning and the end of the era, and human activity may have played no part in the shift. During the African Humid Period, the north part of Africa received higher amounts of sunlight, which drove summer monsoons deeper into the continent. When the climate abruptly shifted back, humans moved to nearby places such as Egypt, and the Sahara returned to the dry conditions found there today.

Now, however, climate change is happening more rapidly than ever before. The majority of scientists agree that a human-driven rise in greenhouse gases is likely the cause. At the same time, human activity and an expanding human population are continuing to destroy and fragment habitats around the world, taking away refuges for vulnerable species while blocking paths for migration.

Climate change is more than just the climate warming. It's also a shift away from normal climactic patterns to dramatic, extreme ones. As climate change continues, heat waves and drought will become more common, while the rain that does fall will tend to come in heavier, more damaging bursts. Changes in the timing of rainfall could have unpredictable results in the desert, while high temperatures and high levels of greenhouse gases can cause shifts in plant communities. In general, the amount of land covered by deserts is predicted to increase.

Some native desert species are adapted to very specific habitats that could shift out from underneath them. Reptiles such as iguanas, lizards, and tortoises are already losing parts of their ranges, leading to falling population numbers. Researchers have noticed that some areas of JTNP have very few young Joshua trees, or even none at all, most likely

The large amount of glaciers melting in Antarctica is one sign of climate change.

> "The world is now using more renewable electric power each year than it is from coal, natural gas and oil put together."[4]
>
> —Ban Ki-moon, former secretary-general of the United Nations, in 2015

CLIMATE ACTION

While progress on fighting climate change has been slower than many would like, there have been encouraging signs. In 2015, 195 nations approved the Paris Climate Accord, an agreement to meet set targets for reducing greenhouse gas emissions within each country.[5] Emissions even fell in many countries between 2014 and 2015, with the highest decline seen in the United States. However, President Trump announced on June 1, 2017, that the United States would back out of the accord. Many other nations remain committed to a sustainable future.

due to a long-lasting drought in the region. Perennial plants go through a particularly vulnerable stage as young seedlings because they need more water to survive than established plants. Worsening droughts are one of the predicted effects of climate change, and researchers are seeing the plight of the Joshua trees as a sign of things to come.

Climate change is caused mostly by forces outside the desert, so the solution must come from outside as well. Many governments recognize that the world is under an unprecedented threat and are grappling with effective responses.

Meanwhile, researchers are monitoring the effect of climate change on desert landscapes. They are cataloging the species currently found in specific places and studying their responses to current and future changes. A better understanding of the processes and problems may help conservationists protect vital habitat for vulnerable species.

OTHER ONGOING CHALLENGES

Scarce water has always been a challenge in the desert, but now the deserts of the world are pressed by people competing for these resources, disrupting water flow and drying up water features. The problem isn't new, but the demand from development and agriculture is dramatically increasing and contributing to desertification. Shrinking glaciers are affecting desert lands that rely on glacial melt water for plant growth. In some places, innovative solutions are popping up. For example, in the Indian region of Ladakh, inventor Sonam Wangchuk is working on artificial glaciers that are frozen in winter and melt in spring to irrigate cropland.

Off-road vehicles continue to be very popular in the deserts of the American Southwest, and in some areas trails are so extensive they've completely stripped away desert vegetation. Some riders continue to venture farther afield, spreading the destruction. But land managers and community groups are continuing to push back against illegal off-roading.

WATER, WATER EVERYWHERE

Approximately 97 percent of water is in the oceans, unusable for humans to drink or irrigate with.[6] Current technology can remove salt from that water, but the process is slow and expensive. A research team led by Dr. Rahul Nair created a sieve that might change that. It promises to remove salt from seawater in a cheaper way. Others are also working on novel ways to derive water from the environment. At the Massachusetts Institute of Technology, researchers have created a prototype that uses solar power to pull water from extremely dry air. It remains to be seen if new sources for water relieve some of the burden on desert lands.

SEQUENCING THE JOSHUA TREE GENOME

Joshua tree seedlings need cool, moist winters and springs to establish themselves, which means they are threatened by a warmer, drier world. The future JTNP may have far fewer Joshua trees because of climate change. Researchers in the United States are trying to change that through a project that will sequence the genome of the Joshua tree. Sequencing a genome is the process of mapping an organism's genetic material.

A genome is the complete set of DNA in an organism. DNA is an organic compound that consists of long sequences of chemical base pairs forming a doubled structure like a microscopic ladder. The genome of a Joshua tree contains approximately three billion base pairs, which would stretch for 9 feet (3 m) if it wasn't coiled up.[7] The sequence of the base pairs forms the codes which make up genes, most of which work by directing the formation of specific proteins in the cell.

After sequencing the genome of one individual tree, the scientists will move on to other individuals. They hope to find genes that are involved with a Joshua tree's adaptations to desert conditions, as well as genes that influence Joshua tree interactions with other Mojave species such as their yucca moth pollinators. Once scientists better understand the genetic diversity in Joshua tree populations, they can develop plans to preserve that diversity. If they identify a population that is particularly well adapted to a warmer and drier world, they can spread seeds from individuals from that population, which will help keep JTNP full of Joshua trees.

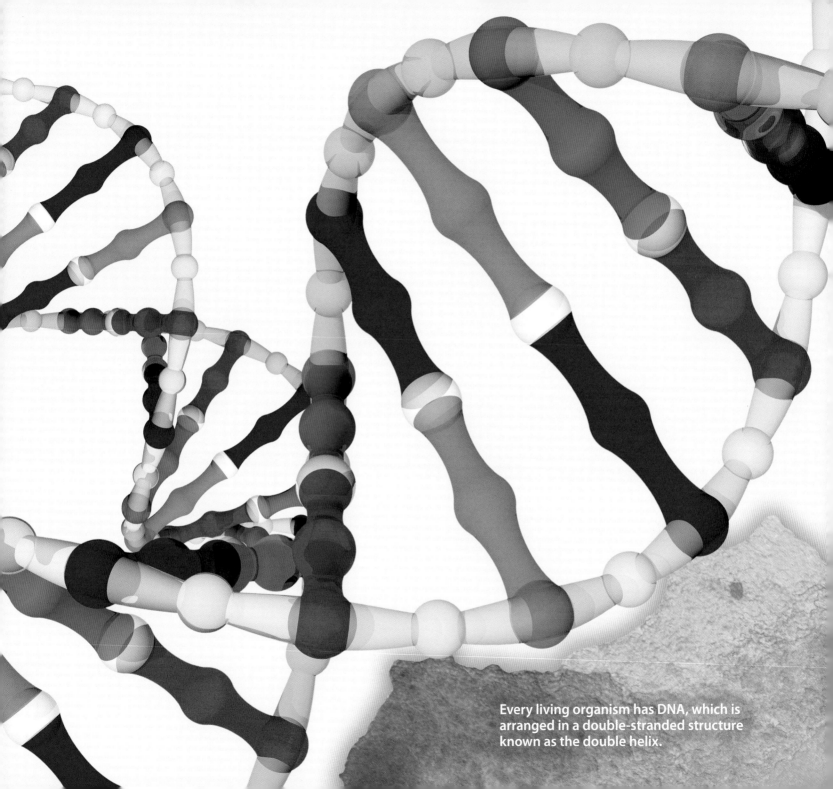

Every living organism has DNA, which is arranged in a double-stranded structure known as the double helix.

Conservation areas, such as Red Rock Canyon in Nevada, protect native species.

Education, fencing, and signage can reduce the spread of off-roading, while trail design can minimize the effects of riders on designated trails.

Deserts have experienced many changes over the last couple of hundred years. As complex ecosystems, desert lands support a variety of unique organisms as well as human livelihoods. Deserts are easily disturbed, having fragile soils as well as life dependent on scarce resources, which human activities make even scarcer. Disturbance can denude deserts and make once-productive land into true wastelands.

Though vulnerable, deserts are also resilient. They can recover on their own, although they recover faster and more fully with human help. People have achieved some big conservation successes in the desert. Large areas have been put under legal protections to prevent further disturbances. Land managers have found ways to protect, enhance, and restore desert biodiversity. While many challenges remain, people can preserve intact desert lands with hard work and innovation. Their efforts will allow the next generation to enjoy and benefit from these lands.

> "Still, there is good news. When attended to, degraded lands recover."[8]
> —*UN Decade for Deserts and the Fight Against Desertification*

UN AGAINST DESERTIFICATION

In 1996, the United Nations Convention to Combat Desertification (UNCCD) came into force with the agreement of more than 180 countries.[9] The convention was set up to address the problems of desertification and degradation of drylands around the world. National Action Programs within each country identify causes of desertification and drought along with practical solutions. The UNCCD helps with research and other support. The UN also declared the years 2010 to 2020 the UN Decade for Deserts and the Fight Against Desertification. This campaign has spread awareness of desertification issues and supported initiatives such as the Great Green Wall, a project working to restore land in Africa.

CAUSE AND EFFECT

SOLUTIONS

Create land preserves

Regulate grazing

Regulate off-road vehicles

Restore desert landscapes

Restore native species

Sustainable agricultural techniques

PROBLEMS

Desertification caused by overgrazing, intensive agriculture, off-road vehicles, and water removal

Close roads

Preserve land from development

Desert loss caused by development

Conserve and restore habitat

Grant legal protections

Captive breeding and release

Plant native species

Biodiversity loss caused by habitat loss, hunting, livestock, and invasive species

Manually remove invasive species

Control invasive species with herbicides

Release biological control agents

Invasive species caused by new introductions and desert disturbances

Reduce emissions

Protect vulnerable species

Climate change caused by rising temperatures and drought

Help species adapt to changes

RESULTS

Ecosystem functions are restored

Erosion is reduced

Deserts begin to heal themselves

Desert productivity increases

Biodiversity increases

Deserts are preserved

Species recover

Desert biodiversity is restored or increased

Ecosystem functions recover

Invasive species are managed

Native species recover

Ecosystem functions are restored

Lower temperatures

Less drought

Biodiversity is protected

ESSENTIAL
FACTS

WHAT IS HAPPENING

Deserts around the world are expanding and becoming more impoverished. In many areas, conservation efforts are helping turn the tide. Restoration projects have helped deserts by reversing damage caused by human activities. Control programs have managed invasive species. Conservation efforts have saved species from extinction and helped biodiversity recover.

THE CAUSES

Overgrazing, agriculture, habitat loss, development, invasive species, pollution, vehicle traffic, and other human activities have reduced native biodiversity and the natural resilience of desert ecosystems.

KEY PLAYERS

People who live, work, or engage in recreation in deserts have a high impact on them, as well as a stake in the ecological services they provide. Government agencies and managers at land preserves often help protect and restore deserts. Zoos participate in captive breeding programs. Volunteers can help desert preserves control invasive species and plant natives. Individual landowners may manage their land in part to promote healthy deserts and rich biodiversity.

WHAT IS BEING DONE TO FIX THE DAMAGE

Lands have been set aside as natural preserves. People have eradicated and controlled invasive species, going after them mechanically, chemically, and biologically. Some native biodiversity has been protected and restored. People have rehabilitated denuded landscapes to restore plant communities and reduce erosion. They have returned water to riparian areas that had been diverted for agriculture and urban areas, facilitating recovery in those areas. Furthermore, people have explored ways to use desert landscapes to raise crops and livestock while protecting biodiversity.

WHAT IT MEANS FOR THE FUTURE

Human activities have changed desert ecosystems around the world, often permanently, but with continued commitments and work toward conservation goals, functioning desert landscapes will continue to support rich, biodiverse ecosystems.

QUOTE

"Viewed from the roadside, the dry land only hints at hidden vitality, but closer examination reveals a giant mosaic of an ecosystem, intensely beautiful and complex."

—*A description of JTNP from* National Parks of the American West

GLOSSARY

ANNUAL
A plant that lives for only one growing season.

AQUIFER
An underground rock formation that contains water or allows water to flow through.

ARID
Extremely dry due to lack of rain or other water sources.

BIODIVERSITY
The variety of life in a particular habitat or ecosystem.

CRYPTOBIOTIC CRUST
A living soil crust that some deserts develop.

DESERTIFICATION
A human-caused process of lands becoming desert or desert lands becoming degraded.

ENDEMIC
A species or organism that is regularly found in a given environment.

GENOME
The complete set of DNA in an organism.

INVASIVE SPECIES
Organisms that arrive in a new ecosystem, take over, and cause harm.

OASIS
A place in the desert with water.

PERENNIAL

Plants that live for more than two years.

RESTORATION ECOLOGY

The science of returning degraded land to a more natural state.

RICHNESS

In ecology, the number of species found in an area.

RIPARIAN

Related to the bank of a river or other body of water.

SUCCULENTS

Plants with fleshy stems or leaves for storing water.

SUSTAINABLE

In ecological terms, a population is sustainable if it can maintain its numbers under the conditions to which it is exposed; for example, a sustainable fishery can be harvested at a reasonable rate and not become depleted.

SYMBIOTIC

Related to two organisms helping each other.

ADDITIONAL RESOURCES

SELECTED BIBLIOGRAPHY

Bainbridge, David A. *A Guide for Desert and Dryland Restoration: New Hope for Arid Lands.* Washington, DC: Island, 2007. Print.

Dilsaver, Larry M. "A History of Preserving the Desert, Administrative History." *National Park Service.* US Department of the Interior, Mar. 2015. Web. 28 June 2017.

Ward, David. *The Biology of Deserts.* Oxford: Oxford UP, 2016. Print.

Webb, Robert H., Lynn F. Fenstermaker, Jill S. Heaton, Debra L. Hughson, Eric V. MacDonald, and David M. Miller, eds. *The Mojave Desert: Ecosystem Processes and Sustainability.* Reno, NV: U of Nevada P, 2009. Print.

FURTHER READINGS

Krebbs, Karen. *Desert Life: A Guide to the Southwest's Iconic Animals and Plants and How They Survive.* Cambridge, MN: Adventure, 2017. Print.

Sibley, Emma. *The Little Book of Cacti and Other Succulents.* London: Quadrille, 2017. Print.

Sneideman, Joshua. *Renewable Energy: Discover the Fuel of the Future.* White River Junction, VT: Nomad, 2016. Print.

ONLINE RESOURCES

To learn more about desert conservation, visit **abdobooklinks.com**. These links are routinely monitored and updated to provide the most current information available.

MORE INFORMATION

For more information on this subject, contact or visit the following organizations:

Arizona-Sonora Desert Museum

2021 North Kinney Road
Tucson, AZ 85743
520-883-2702
desertmuseum.org

The Arizona-Sonora Desert Museum runs research and conservation programs.

California Wilderness Coalition

1814 Franklin Street
Suite 510
Oakland, CA 94612
510-451-1450
calwild.org

The California Wilderness Coalition supports permanent protection for natural areas in California.

SOURCE NOTES

CHAPTER 1. JOSHUA TREE NATIONAL PARK

1. "Joshua Tree: Park Statistics." *National Park Service.* Department of the Interior, 24 May 2016. Web. 24 Aug. 2017.

2. "Joshua Tree: Birds." *National Park Service.* Department of the Interior, 4 Apr. 2017. Web. 24 Aug. 2017.

3. "Joshua Tree: Animals." *National Park Service.* Department of the Interior, 4 Apr. 2017. Web. 24 Aug. 2017.

4. "Joshua Tree: Insects, Spiders, Centipedes, Millipedes." *National Park Service.* Department of the Interior, 26 Apr. 2017. Web. 24 Aug. 2017.

5. "Joshua Tree: Wilderness." *National Park Service.* Department of the Interior, 29 June 2016. Web. 24 Aug. 2017.

6. Don Laine and Barbara Laine. *Frommer's National Parks of the American West.* 8th ed. Hoboken, NJ: John Wiley and Sons, 2012. Print. 279.

7. Robert H. Webb, et al, eds. *The Mojave Desert: Ecosystems Processes and Sustainability.* Reno, NV: U of Nevada, 2009. Print. 393.

8. "Joshua Tree National Park Sees Record Visitation in 2016." *National Park Service.* Department of the Interior, 17 Jan. 2017. Web. 24 Aug. 2017.

9. Lary M. Dilsaver. "A History of Preserving the Desert, Administrative History." Twentynine Palms, CA: Joshua Tree National Park, 2015. Web. 294.

10. "Yucca." *The Plant List.* The Plant List, 2013. Web. 24 Aug. 2017.

11. David Sadava, et al. *Life: The Science of Biology Volume 2: Evolution, Diversity, and Ecology.* 9th ed. Sunderland, MA: Sinauer Associates, 2011. 544, 1232. *Google Book Search.* Web. 24 Aug. 2017.

CHAPTER 2. WHAT IS A DESERT?

1. Michael Allaby. *Deserts (Ecosystems).* New York: Facts on File, 2001. Print.

2. "What is a Desert?" *USGS.* US Geological Survey, 18 Dec. 2001. Web. 24 Aug. 2017.

3. Ronald Peel and Jeffrey Gritzner. "Sahara." *Encyclopedia Britannica.* Encyclopedia Britannica, 2017. Web. 24 Aug. 2017.

4. "Death Valley: Weather." *National Park Service.* Department of the Interior, 22 Apr. 2016. Web. 24 Aug. 2017.

5. David Ward. *The Biology of Deserts.* 2nd ed. Oxford: Oxford University, 2016. Print. 5.

6. "Types of Deserts." *USGS.* US Geological Survey, 29 Oct. 1997. Web. 24 Aug. 2017.

7. Arizona-Sonoran Desert Museum. *A Natural History of the Sonoran Desert.* Oakland, CA: University of California, 2015. Print. 12.

8. "Death Valley: Wildflowers." *National Park Service.* Department of the Interior, 9 Mar. 2017. Web. 24 Aug. 2017.

9. Jay W. Sharp. "Mesquite Tree." *Desert USA.* Desert USA, 2017. Web. 24 Aug. 2017.

10. "Spring Ecosystems." *Springs Stewardship Institute.* Museum of Northern Arizona, n.d. Web. 24 Aug. 2017.

CHAPTER 3. HUMAN FOOTPRINT IN THE DESERT

1. David A. Bainbridge. *A Guide for Desert and Dryland Restoration: New Hope for Arid Lands*. Washington, DC: Island, 2007. Print. 3.

2. "Frequently Asked Questions (FAQ)." *UN Convention to Combat Desertification*. UNCCD Secretariat, n.d. Web. 24 Aug. 2017.

3. "Desertification Land Degradation and Drought (DLDD) – Some Global Facts and Figures." *UN Convention to Combat Desertification*. UNCCD Secretariat, n.d. Web. 24 Aug. 2017.

4. Ibid.

5. Matthew Leivas Sr. "Desert National Monuments Represent a Shared Connection to the Land." *Press-Enterprise*. Press-Enterprise, 25 June 2017. Web. 24 Aug. 2017.

CHAPTER 4. PROTECTING LAND

1. Stuart Chape, et al. "Measuring the Extent and Effectiveness of Protected Areas as an Indicator for Meeting Global Biodiversity Targets." *Philosophical Transactions of the Royal Society B*. 360 (2005): 443-455, 450. *Royal Society Publishing*. Web. 24 Aug. 2017.

2. "California Desert Protection Act of 1994—History." *California Desert Protection Act*. Joshua Tree National Park Council for the Arts, 2014. Web. 24 Aug. 2017.

3. Ibid.

4. "S. 21 (103rd): California Desert Protection Act of 1994." *GovTrack*. GovTrack, 8 Oct. 1994. Web. 24 Aug. 2017.

5. Lary M. Dilsaver. "A History of Preserving the Desert, Administrative History." Twentynine Palms, CA: Joshua Tree National Park, 2015. Web. 173-174.

6. Merrit Kennedy. "Photos: Obama Declares 3 New National Monuments in California Desert." *NPR*. NPR, 12 Feb. 2016. Web. 24 Aug. 2017.

7. "Namibia: How Communities Led a Conservation Success Story." *WWF*. World Wildlife Fund, 12 Apr. 2011. Web. 24 Aug. 2017.

8. "Wildlife and National Parks." *Ministry of Environment and Tourism*. Ministry of Environment and Tourism Namibia, 2017. Web. 24 Aug. 2017.

9. "WCS/ZSL-Led Study Documents Catastrophic Collapse of Wildlife in Sahara Desert." *Wildlife Conservation Society*. Wildlife Conservation Society, 3 Dec. 2013. Web. 24 Aug. 2017.

10. Alexandra E. Petri. "Cheetahs Are Dangerously Close to Extinction." *National Geographic*. National Geographic Society, 27 Dec. 2016. Web. 24 Aug. 2017.

SOURCE
NOTES *CONTINUED*

11. Ibid.

12. Mohammad S. Farhadinia, et al. "The Critically Endangered Asiatic Cheetah *Acinonyx jubatus venaticus* in Iran: A Review of Recent Distribution, and Conservation Status." *Biodiversity and Conservation* 26.5(May 2017): 1027-1046. *Springer Link*. Web. 24 Aug. 2017.

CHAPTER 5. TACKLING INVASIVE SPECIES

1. David Ward. *The Biology of Deserts*. 2nd ed. Oxford: Oxford University, 2016. Print. 250.

2. "Saguaro: Invasive Plants." *National Park Service*. Department of the Interior, 21 July 2017. Web. 24 Aug. 2017.

3. "Tamarisk Biocontrol in California." *Riparian Invasion Research Laboratory*. UCSB, 2012. Web. 24 Aug. 2017.

CHAPTER 6. RETURNING DESERT BIODIVERSITY

1. Steve Conner. "Desert Life Threatened by Climate Change and Human Exploitation." *Independent*. Independent, 4 June 2006. Web. 24 Aug. 2017.

2. "Succulent Karoo." *Critical Ecosystem Partnership Fund*. Conservation International, 2016. Web. 24 Aug. 2017.

3. David Ward. *The Biology of Deserts*. 2nd ed. Oxford: Oxford University, 2016. Print. 1.

4. Christine Dell'Amore. "Arabian 'Unicorn' Leaps Out of Near Extinction." *National Geographic*. National Geographic Society, 17 June 2011. Web. 24 Aug. 2017.

5. "California Condor Recovery Program: 2016 Annual Population Status." *Fish and Wildlife Service*. Department of the Interior, 2016. Web. 24 Aug. 2017.

6. Diana Lutz. "The Secret Lives of the Wild Asses of the Negev." *The Source*. Washington University in St. Louis, 27 Mar. 2013. Web. 24 Aug. 2017.

7. Paul Tolme. "Counting Sheep." *National Wildlife Federation*. National Wildlife Federation. 1 June 2008. Web. 24 Aug. 2017.

8. "Endangered Willow Flycatcher Recovering Slowly, Efforts Continue." *Tamarisk Coalition*. Tamarisk Coalition, 18 Mar. 2015. Web. 24 Aug. 2017.

9. David Louis. "Conservation Plan Being Sought for Mohave Desert Tortoise." *Havasu News*. Havasu News. 8 Feb. 2017. Web. 24 Aug. 2017.

CHAPTER 7. RESTORING DESERT LANDS

1. Alexis Marie Adams. "'Restoration Economy' Strives to Protect Pollinators, Create Jobs." *Scientific American*. Scientific American, 21 Nov. 2016. Web. 24 Aug. 2017.

2. Brian Howard Clark. "Saving the Colorado River Delta, One Habitat at a Time." *National Geographic*. National Geographic Society, 15 Dec. 2014. Web. 24 Aug. 2017.

CHAPTER 8. SUSTAINING USE

1. "Why Now?" *UN Decade For Deserts and the Fight Against Desertification*. UN, n.d. Web. 24 Aug. 2017.

2. Kathryn Wells. "Australian Farming and Agriculture—Grazing and Cropping." *Australian Government*. Australian Government, 31 Mar. 2015. Web. 24 Aug. 2017.

3. Lauren Hull. "Wild Rabbits: Working Together to Get Results." *Landcare Australia*. Landcare Australia, 2017. Web. 24 Aug. 2017.

CHAPTER 9. THE FUTURE DESERT

1. "Ice Ages." *BBC*. BBC, 2017. Web. 24 Aug. 2017.

2. Bettina Boxall. "Interior Department Signs Blueprint for Renewable Energy Development in the California Desert." *LA Times*. LA Times, 14 Sept. 2016. Web. 24 Aug. 2017.

3. Peter B. deMenocal and Jessica E. Tierney. "Green Sahara: African Humid Periods Paced by Earth's Orbital Changes." *Nature Education Knowledge* 3.10 (2012). *Nature Education Knowledge Project*. Web. 24 Aug. 2017.

4. "'Journey Towards Bold Climate Action is at a Critical Moment,' UN General Assembly Told." *Sustainable Development Goals*. United Nations, 29 June 2015. Web. 24 Aug. 2017.

5. Coral Davenport. "Nations Approve Landmark Climate Accord in Paris." *New York Times*. New York Times, 12 Dec. 2015. Web. 24 Aug. 2017.

6. "How Much Water Is in the Ocean?" *National Ocean Service*. NOAA, 6 July 2017. Web 24 Aug. 2017.

7. J. T. Gadmin. "Getting to the Essence of a Joshua Tree: DNA Extraction." *Joshua Tree Genome*. Joshua Tree Genome, 6 Sept. 2016. Web. 24 Aug. 2017.

8. "United Nations Decade for Deserts and the Fight against Desertification [Brochure]." Bonn, Germany: UNCCD Secretariat. *UN*. Web. 24 Aug. 2017.

9. "About the Convention." *UN Convention to Combat Desertification*. UNCCD, n.d. Web. 24 Aug. 2017.

INDEX

ABOUT THE
AUTHOR

Clara MacCarald is a freelance writer with a master's degree in biology. Before becoming a writer, she helped study wildlife in forests, deserts, and prairies. She has written several books for kids on science and history and belongs to both the National Association of Science Writers and the Society of Children's Book Writers and Illustrators.